To Riley,

Believe that you can do Anything!

Lisa Welden

Lola Gose to School

Scripture quotations, unless otherwise indicated, are taken from The Holy Bible, King James Version, Cambridge, 1769. Used by permission. All rights reserved.

The opinions expressed by the author are not necessarily those of Fountain of Life Publisher's House.

Published by Fountain of Life Publisher's House
P. O. Box 922612, Norcross, Georgia, 30010 Phone: 404.936.3989

Fountain of Life Publisher's House is committed to excellence in the publishing industry. The company reflects the philosophy established by the founders based on Psalms 68:11, "The Lord gave the word and great was those of the company of those who published it."

Cover Design & Illustrated by: Niaren Binford
Editor: Debra Richards

ISBN: 978-1548987497

October 23, 2017

To the Parents:

Handicapable, Lola Goes to School, is the second children's book from the Handicapable series. This book is about a little girl named Lola, who is wheelchair bound, experiencing school for the first time. She meets her classmates, who are also physically challenged and they form a very necessary bond. Lola is reacquainted with her friend Zack, who as a result of her encouraging him, now shares her positivity. Together they ultimately confront the bullies of the school, in effort to enlighten them and change their negative mind sets. The purpose of this book is to have the conversation about bullying and evoke thought about the solution.

Hi, my name is Lola. I'm five years old and today is my first day of school. I'm so excited because I get to go to school like my big sisters.

Mommy will help me decide which dress to wear. I hope I can wear one of my princess dresses. This is a special day and I have to look nice.

Mommy said, "It doesn't matter what you wear. Just be yourself Lola, and I'm sure you will be fine. First impressions are important, but who you are on the inside is more important."

"Hurry up Lola, you don't want to be late on your first day of school. Your sisters are waiting. This is not the time to make an America's Next Top Model entrance, Lil Diva," said Daddy.

My family has a special van made for my princess mobile. Daddy opens the side door and presses a button that makes the lift go down. I roll my chair on the lift and it rises so that I can roll inside the van. My sisters sit in the back of the van with me.

The lady standing at the entrance door says, "Hello, my name is Mrs. Greene. I am your daughter's teacher." Mommy and Daddy shake her hand and smile. Daddy said, "This is Lola." "Pleased to meet you Lola. I really like your chair. I have never seen a chair as pretty as yours," said Mrs. Greene.

My classroom is big with bright colors. There are letters and numbers on the walls and blocks and puzzles on the tables. The back of the room looks like a kitchen with plates, pots and pans. I even see little closets and beds near the kitchen area. I guess this is supposed to be like home since we will be spending a lot of time here.

I can't wait to make friends. A girl wearing a pretty yellow dress came in the classroom. She is not in a chair like I am. She has something helping her stand. It has wheels on it and she pushes it to walk.

I smiled and said, "Hi my name is Lola. What is your name?" "My name is Isabella," she replied. Lola asked, "Do you have a name for your wheels?" "Nope, it is just my walker," said Isabella. I told Isabella that we have to come up with a cool name for her walker like I have for my princess mobile.

Before I knew it, Isabella zoomed to the other side of the classroom and came back with crayons and paper. Isabella has very strong arms. She might be able to beat me in a race. I told Isabella that I believe I will walk one day. Maybe she will too, since she is already standing with a walker.

A boy came into the classroom. I asked him his name, and he said, "It's Mathew." He looked like he wanted to say more, but it took him a long time to say the words. I touched his arm and said, "It's okay, take your time and say what's on your mind."

Mathew picked up a pencil and pad. In just a few minutes, he had drawn a picture of me and my princess mobile. With a surprised look on my face, I said, "Wow, I can't believe how fast you drew that picture." He smiled and said, "It's for you."

The door opened, and guess who came in? It was Zack. Zack is the boy who I met at the Hope House Recreation Center. He was in a wheelchair like me, but mine was nicer than his. Now he was in a chair that looked like a racing car. It even had racing stripes and lights on the wheels. I gave Zack a fist pump because I was happy to see him.

He told me that during the summer, he joined a basketball team named Team Expanding Limits. Zack smiled and said, "I listened to what you told me about being happy with what I can do instead of being sad about what I can't do."

The day was going by fast. It was time to go to the schoolyard for recess. The schoolyard was filled with children and teachers. Isabella and Mathew looked scared. Zack and I led the way and went out first. We didn't realize that the other kids were watching us.

33

They called us names and laughed at us. Some kids were pointing at our chairs and Isabella's walker. They made fun of the way Mathew talked. One boy called Isabella robot girl and said that Zack and I were transformers.

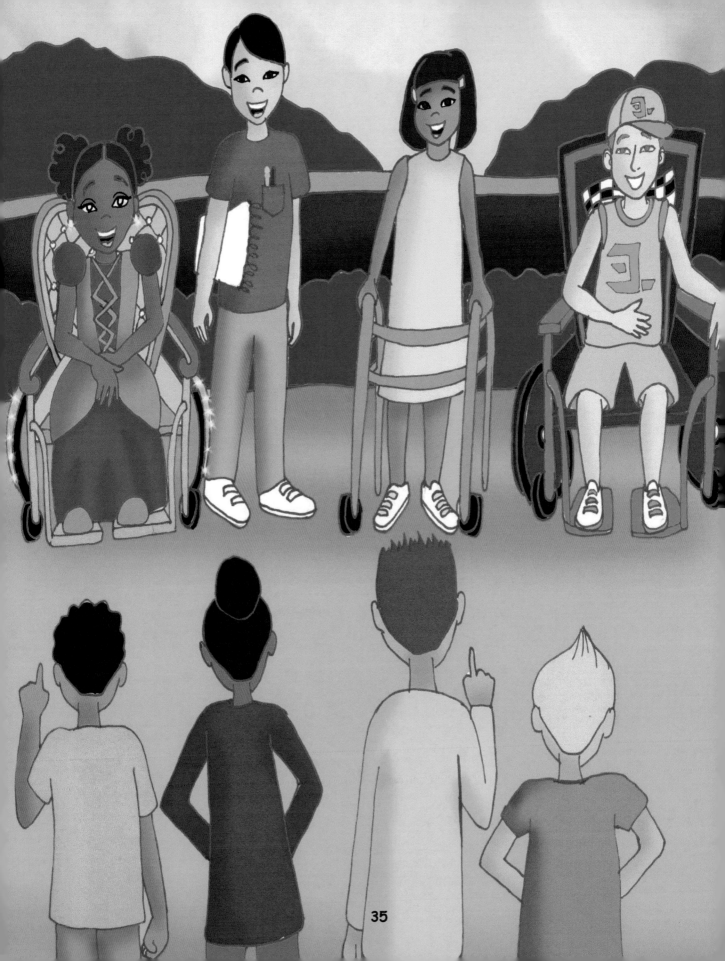

I said to them, "Why are you being so mean to us? We are not bothering you. We are different from you but we are special in our own way. It's not nice to treat us like we don't have feelings. You just don't understand us and I think that scares you."

Lola said, "I am so proud of the way we stood up to the bullies. They needed to know that we are strong and smart just like they are. We will not be afraid of them anymore."

The four of us moved away from the group of kids. We were laughing and playing with each other. I watched Zack pop wheelies in his chair. Isabella and Mathew were playing patty cake. We were having so much fun, that the other kids began to watch us play.

A few of the kids came over to us. One of the boys put his hand out to shake my hand and said, "You're right. We shouldn't be mean to you. We can see that you can do cool stuff just like us. You just have your own way of doing it. I'm sorry for the way we acted."

"You must be pretty strong to do those tricks with your chair," said the boy. He looked at Mathew's picture and said, "Dude, you can really draw. Can you show me how to draw like you? We promise not to make fun of you again."

"You have courage out of this world, speaking up for your friends. We weren't thinking about your feelings. Can we all be friends?" the boy asked. His hands were clasped together as he dropped to his knees pleading to Lola.

Lola turned, looked at her friends and said, "What do you all think? Will we forgive them?" They all shook their heads and said, "Yes!"

Lola said, "Just to show you how strong we really are, watch this." Lola held on to both sides of her chair and slowly stood up. The children began to cheer, clap and give each other high fives. She shouted, "WE ARE HANDICAPABLE!"

Special Dedication

This book is dedicated to my grandson Jason. I love you with all my heart.

Philippians 4:13

"For I can do all things through Christ, who gives me strength."

Acknowledgements

Thank you to my Lord and Savior, who is the author and finisher of my faith. Thanks to my husband, Creighton, for loving me through everything. Thanks to my sons, Kyle and Corey, for their love and for bringing out the best in me. I would like to thank my late parents, Edward and Blossom, for never allowing me to give up or make excuses. Thank you to my sisters, Jackie, Debbie and Cathy, for encouraging me to follow my dreams. Thank you to my aunt, uncles, nieces, nephews, cousins and in-laws, for believing in me.

A special thanks to my dear friends who mean more to me than words can say. Thanks to my 911 family for being loyal and spreading the Handicapable message. Thank you to my Pastor, Reverend, Dr. Robert Waterman, First Lady Lola, and my Antioch Baptist Church family, for their continued support and prayers. I attribute all my accomplishments and success to the intricate part that each and every one of you have played throughout this journey.

Lisa Weldon

Contact Lisa Weldon www.booksbylisaw.com

Email: booksbylisaw@gmail.com

Fountain of Life Publisher's House

www.pariceparker.biz

Made in the USA
Columbia, SC
27 March 2018